Oil on Canvas Painting - 1986 - by Ayad Gharbawi

Scruples of the Devil

Ayad Gharbawi

authorHOUSE®

AuthorHouse™ UK Ltd.
500 Avebury Boulevard
Central Milton Keynes, MK9 2BE
www.authorhouse.co.uk
Phone: 08001974150

First published by AuthorHouse   8/7/2012

ISBN: 978-1-4772-2181-5 (sc)
ISBN: 978-1-4772-2182-2 (e)

Table of Contents

2010 – Damascus, Syria

Location: Desert Shore, Bitterly Cold Night, next to strong waves from the ocean.

Characters: Man ((M) and his Lover, a Woman (W).

— — — — — — — — — — — — — — — —

W: "Search as I forever do, in manifold ways unknown, I seek but to love thee, and the meagre goodness from Life, with steely ardour - my armour faithful."

M: "Alone I may be, and still, yes I love thee; these days heavy are and beset I am by burdensome trivialities, but I remain trusting, though my corner so narrow remain."

W: "My Love! Your speech I hear aloud and thine lips I live within and yet, my Love, all Solitude I am. Man! I am unaided! In this journey of sinful thorns, my love, in this unforgiving journey, this blurred odyssey, I stand alone".

M: "This trial you speak of, but I do know of it well; so, listen then: within the strength of trusted togetherness we can plough on, though everlasting harm shall do its spiteful tricks, warm to our united truth shall we remain."

W: (Surprised) "O! My love! This thought I cannot hear! My life, my destiny, is but mine. And all have their own solitary roads of jagged rocks to embrace, like it we or not. We heartbreaking earthly sad beasts, either fiercely clutch at integrity, or we do let it go to perish away."

M: (Confused) "My Love! I do hear, I do hear. But when Times decide on burdening us, what then can we achieve? To face Reality within the frail arms of solitude is to ignore, to refuse the severe threats of repulsive grins."

(Silence)

M: (Passionately) "O! My sweet! Only in us, can we envelope, through joined, clasped warmth can we be as one united! The screams that so truly are meant to slice us on, only we, our Unity, can destroy. For mine eyes can only find sleep in your ears, and it is so - for otherwise nothing and no one can be."

W: (Angry) "My Passion too is bubbling for thine bewildered ears. Am I not your soul? Do we not suffer as one? Do we not reflect as one? Am I not your lover true? Is not our warmth not weighty to our fickle bones?"

(Silence)

W: (Passionate) "But, Lover, this much ought I to formally declare unto thee: For our eyes, and all eyes, envision unequally at one another. Till eternity, in its casual, indifferent flicker, snatches at us all wretched mortals, the gazes from lords to paupers remain veritably mismatched. O my passion! My woeful heart! These words I thunder forth defines love unfeigned, and what mine eyes do pour out unto thine ears is authenticity true.

(Silence)

W: (Passionately) "What joined mem'ries you choose to caress may possess thee, but your exactness for what love is to you, doth not dwell in mine mind. What tears, what weepings you do, fall stormily upon thine own soul's wildernesses. You choose to be chained by changing visions and indefinite sentiments of light weight – though so poignant at the moment they veritably are?"

M: (Inquiring) "My love! I cherish thee; where hast thou been in thine mind, for now ye talk of that truth you relate to in your heart. Your pronouncements, what depths I do feel! Can it perchance be that my passion has strayed our winds far from me?"

W: "No, my love! Why is anger, I feel, lush on thine tongue?"

M: (Surprised and Frightened) "Anger! I am too distant from that affliction! But yes, I feel my words make only for unstable murmurs in my breath."

W: (Quietly) "Then, do tell me, lover, who do your murmurs betray - myself or yourself then?"

M: (Quietly) "Perhaps so, perhaps so. But my anxiety wilfully demands of me to eradicate your vision."

W: (Firmly) "You answer naught from my undemanding question. Or, are mine meanings too violent for you? What aches thee?"

M: (Passionately) "My sweet! In so many moments, I created mysterious planets for thee! Bizarre worlds of contrasts and opposites and musical words of antiquity and sensual ravines. My love! I, my soul, my life, my inner deepest breath, tempted as I am by Fates' inscrutable cruelties to ashamedly yield, I have yet always expressed to mine eyes' heart, though they be in bleak darkness, to faithfully fight without pause all shades of vice and still yet - with loving integrity; I have stood with arms of righteousness and love for thee up and never down! Yes, sincere good and venal ill remain joined in life for all to feel, but you knew it was not for me to disentangle them. And so, I pronounce unto thee, still, and yet ever and ever more, my love for thee, though still beholding a thousand mountains before me, I remain sturdy for thee; I remain undisturbed by burly laws, and by exotic dictums, I stand fierce and unhurt, save in your absence."

W: (With Sadness) "My beloved, your vivid voice stabs the falsehoods for thee, and I say unto thee, unto thee your excessive and unreasonable chains, and for myself my unreasonable and extreme chains remain."

M: (Shocked) "But I burden thee with no steely chains, nor verbal fetters! For naught I produce for thee save grace, passion and freedom to love for us both to be in Unity Sacred! Dost thou embrace my visions as 'shackles', then 'tis better we agree to class that which we are as but madness! Hear me, for my tears now must truly change their colours!"

W: (Determined) "Your feverish hands clutch only upon mine erratic wings!"

M: (Anger) "Never! Never! For I clutch only to destroy all malevolence; as for thee, Lady of the purest, untouched, guarded, secluded Ponds, I seek to unshackle for you the scattered, scared shadows that yearn for thine sovereignty. And what is this 'sovereignty' but our Sacred Union? What curse deemest you I impose? Do you equal my purest passions with atrocities? Murmur unto mine ears, your clearest love for me."

W: "Ah! You enquire of me my 'sincerity' for thee? What demands!"

(Silence)

M: "I see naught but heaving forests of love betwixt us, and yet, you discover my words being 'demanding'?"

W: (Drily) "Perchance, your visions are indistinct and ever more blurred, through these years cannot be ignored."

M: (Begging) "My love! All mine life, though it be lengthy, I fought most venal tyranny, and for this moment, you question my righteousness?"

W: (Indignantly) "I have been plunged into seas hostile and I have plunged in a thousand miles of inert minds troubled beyond conceivable comprehension and I have yet to have my Right for my own greedy, ravenous flesh to be vigorously and forcefully embraced by sensuality and serenity. Yes, I do love thee, and yet in our union, as in all unions, I have been adorned with naught, save snickering, gossiping scenes of festive balls, games, chatter and farewells, themselves festooned within silly and sincerely stupid smiles and frowns, and shallow tears and never ending ludicrous chatter unworthy of monkeys conversing. I have met programmed rows of pats, respect and all other so-called decent intents and gestures, but, where, lover that you are of mine, where does my personal heart, throb and manically vibrate, save in your heavenly imaginations?"

(Silence)

W: (Quietly but Determinedly) "My love! I truly thee love and with passions, I tell you, of proportions of precise exactitudes; in your eyes I have witnessed symphonies of exquisiteness; and, I of thee ask: where dwelleth your own love for myself in thine body?"

(Silence)

W: (Passionate) "Do you recognise the changing structures that form this, that I name 'My Love'? In my solitude eternal, I do evermore and always do pause, and be pensive, and be thinking of questions, such as 'where', 'why', 'when' 'how', and 'which' should be my path; I am forever and ever more searching, seeking the heavens of every corner, and the irritable tempests, within my changing self as they themselves do try to seek me, and we forever, through inconceivable murkiness, do try to assemble the everlasting entirety of these disorganized puzzles into some measure of comprehensible cohesion that 'I' am. That is how the 'I' you love is forever changing and thereby formulating itself, and within all these meandering passions, and endless errors, where am I to feel thee? Where? And where do you seek me? In which land? In which forest? You trivialise my beingness as you focus upon my lands as being that which so effortless to find, and yet, you are much too distant from an understanding of my conflicting, emerging civilisations."

(Silence)

W: (Passionate) If the utterance 'Never' is pathetic for thee, then allow me to introduce you to my latest heart: for it screams out that single, protracted utterance! Never! My love, these winds of raging wraths, both within and outside by flesh, must and can only be annihilated by mine own sincerities — were I not to play against my own self. My uncontrolled desires and, yes, thirsty manic passions can only be tempered and thoroughly satiated to the utter brim, by mine own loving, sources of pleasure, my own uncontrollable ecstasies. As for the rest of bodily pleasures, my own erroneous words, speeches and utterances can only be severed and sliced by my tranquillity."

M: (Resigned) "I hear thine words. Do not abandon me. Do not destroy our civilisation of justice."

W: "What we share, the bonds, are enjoyment. Listen though to mine lips: enjoyment is what - when it is to be compared with convulsive ecstatic quivers of satisfaction?"

M: (Puzzled) "And what of all our journeys to attain that unity? For all that, is it to be of mere insignificance? And if that be your truth, for what then did we toil and labour for unity of minds and bodies?"

W: (Laughing) "Did you understand from Life itself, that here it was, grandly to proclaim its furtive faces unto thine own awaiting face?! "

M: (Baffled) "It was so far too plain and vastly clear unto me these sceneries we faced before our loving bodies."

W: "Yes, and I too, did see them with thee. Our four eyes, did see unity for that flicker of time. How true you speak! But, time clocked on, I saw you as you stood there, moving nowhere, unawares that it was your duty to squash onwards whatever vile breaths faced us."

M: (Desperate) "And did I not? Did I abandon thee in these crushing paths?"

W: (Accusing) "No, you did not. Never, once did you abandon me. I ask of thee; for what sense do we feel a need for a continuation of these gruelling marches? For unity? For love? Or, is love unity? Was that and is this our reason for us to carry on with these shackles?"

M: "For assuredly, yes, and more yes, I tell thee! Toil and gruelling dawns, and unbearable evenings and the whitest of nights are all for the sacred attainment of that heavenly summit of joy I name as blessed 'Love'."

W: (Assured) "And, Sire, what if my nerves, blood and bodily hunger tell thee in truth that we, all of us, need no longer, and need never in truth, to undertake these paths, for we find naught that nourishes us at the blessed summit of your definition of what 'Love' is?"

M: (Confused & Sad) "So, I falter here and now upon understanding your speech; do I reason from thee that our loving days in unity are frivolously bygone now?"

W: (Calmly & Gracefully) "Do the wandering birds, and do the blind bats, and do the reckless storms, and do the blindly, raging waves and do the supremely arrogant oceans eternally march on in but one direction only with the savage passage of time within their particular lives? You did pronounce that you built planets for our unity; well then, did you not view how planets endlessly revolve along the same path?"

(Pause)

W: (Calmly & with Dignity) "For, Sire, I am not as a Planet - could you not feel that throughout our journeys? You endlessly query and question 'who' it is that 'I' am? Well, I speak this much on myself; I am as the birds, and the bats, and the storms and the waves and the oceans."

M: (Angry) "Woman! I can only then tell of thee that you are naught but feuding clutter and violent disarray!"

W: (Unconcerned) "Those are your words. Not mine. Speak for what you wish, Sire."

M: (Angry) "And I stand here, before thee, in anger – nay, more, more! In fury!"

W: (Laughing) "For what? For the deeds that created but sticky, and grimy grains of sand for the undoubted pleasure our eyes?"

M: "And so you label our truths, our love so much! Fair indeed, you speak, Woman of Justice."

W: (Arrogantly) "Man! Express your delights for your own delights. And, alas, there the circle and reality ends – and it ends only for you. That is one morsel of truth for you to ponder. What we 'created' and what we 'loved' was never and never, ever be the same for you as it is for me. Are you a sincere believer that your personal vision is the same sight all other seeing creatures envision?"

M: (Angry) "Woman, you enrage me! Your arrogance is drenching thine rags."

W: (Sarcastic) "Tis the Man with no reason who allows his breath and words to be a veritable cesspool of fuming stenches!"

M: "But I, that I am, no longer can define your content."

W: (Pointedly) "Precisely, Man, precisely. Perhaps, now you have come closer to the vulnerable shores of reality!"

M: (Confused) "Do you express that you are ever varying and so for that reason there is not a one unified you?"

W: (Calmly) "For we are all 'varying', to borrow your word – if you do so allow me, Sire. There was never 'unity' of soul, nor mind, nor self, nor of any one personality. This, I desire, that you may understand."

M: (Aghast) "Then if that be your truth and then, are we naught but multitudes of ever changing confusions, Lady of the Desert?"

W: (Calmly) "Yes and no! For those who are muscular and full of fertile vigour in their flesh, and in their intellects, and those that are severely and strictly scholastic, then they do need and they can succeed in time, in their never ending struggle to bring together the mutually antagonistic factions of that which constitutes our beingness. And, as for the dense brained soulless beings, then, it is equally veritably true that, a descent into madness can be rapidly produced, since from their erratic constituents, they cannot attract together these antagonistic and mutually-hating emotions in some vision of cohesion, and thus mayhem can be fashioned."

(Silence)

M: (Calmly) "So, pray do tell me, where does Love and Justice and Truth and Morality stand in your universe?"

W: (Serenely) "That has been mine desire to hear the words being produced from your lips, Man!"

(Pause)

W: "So, now perhaps, your sight may be getting clearer, for your question is certainly apt. Foremost, we pathetic mortals, we the be are forever slimy specks of sand that crumbles, must necessarily seek to survive and flourish within whatever forest, desert, meadow we find ourselves cast upon."

M: (Startled) "At what cost, Woman? At the expense of Morality?"

W: (Rapidly) "Yes and no."

M: (Shocked) "Horrendous! How can you spout out such filth?"

W: (Quietly) "Restrain your stupidities, and give more room to your intelligence, Sire."

(Silence)

W: (Gracefully) "In times of trouble, what can Man do when he be forced to embrace evil, even though he finds the act of the embrace loathsome, but he does what he does for the truth of his vital existence to continue. Only when he need never embrace vile, and then allows himself to commit the act, then he is for certainty to incur the everlasting wrath of God. Evil is thus never one truth to be utterly rejected, perchance you may now see. ”

M: (Calm but Tired) "I follow your words and their ideas therein."

W: (Gracefully) "When you talk to me on Man and everlasting, conflicting changes within that self-same creature, I tell you with all the earnestness that I possess, of what God has scattered and endowed upon me; for this beast, we all call in unity Man, this creature has far too many a numberless number of mutually self-contradicting, distrusting, loving, hating, inspiring and a never ending number of feelings and emotions that are in constant flow and change – as in any rapid river descending unto its eventual destination, which in its case, is the sea, while in our case, it is Death itself for sure."

M: (Despair) "And how can this beast 'love' anyone within this welter of confusion?"

W: (Rapidly) "He cannot!"

M: (Rapidly, Begging) "But Man and Woman do love with bristling passions! Do you deny that, Woman?!"

W: (Calmly, eyes downwards looking) "Yes, and no. Since the beast has needs, based on his vastly intricate constituents, to 'love' his fellow beast, he imagines and believes in his imagination that he is really in a situation of 'love' and that – as you put it, is 'bristling with passion'."

M: (Softly) "So, Woman, it all but illusions, you speak?"

W: (Sorrowfully) "Yes, and no. I tell you that as far the 'loving' beast, since he genuinely believes that this is 'love', then it truly becomes 'love' for him. But, as far as the wider truth of reality expresses itself in its manifold manners, we sadly know that he is nowhere near 'love' and that he is being but his mere self – which is to say, being typically delusional!"

M: (Exasperated) "My Lord! Everything for you is "yes and no"; you are yourself nothing but energy that is contradictory. I mean to ask you, as per my last question - is Man in love or is he not in love and yet, before me, here, I see you produce yet ever more paradoxically senseless answers! Have you nothing that lies purely straight before thine eyes and mind?"

W: (Impatient) "Alas, you Man, if your mind is not as endowed as it may need to be, then the fault is surely not to be mine, is it? That is a question for you to ask our dear God upon your particular meeting with Him."

M: (Angry) "Are you daring to speak that I am daft, you foolish Woman?"

W: (Amused) "Precisely. Well, actually not precisely. Far more than 'daft'."

M: (Sarcastic) "Anyone who does not agree with you is dim?"

W: (Laughing sarcastically) "Man, what a senseless fool you indeed are. I never have spoken words that anyone who is in 'disagreement' with me must be dim. However, and this sentence is certainly for you: I do say that if Man is incapable of understanding my words, then he must be not dissimilar to our cousins, the apes."

M: (Pleading) "Woman! I ask you, can Love be - or can it not be?"

W: (Subdued) "Permit me, Man, how do you explain unto me what 'Love' is?"

M: (In anger and pride) "What is Love? You ask that of me? I, a warrior all my decades, fighting furiously and fighting passionately against all oppressors, against all evil-doers, and you say to me what is 'Love'?"

W: (Inquisitive) "You have expressed to me that you have fought all your brief life against injustice, and that is noble by all standards. But where is it that I am meant to witness you finding this Love of thine?"

M: "Love is the struggle itself against tyranny itself, do you happen to see naught but veils and mists and fogs?"

W: (Sarcastic) "So, if I choose to fight against tyrannical rulers, then I produce 'Love' from my actions?"

M: (Frantic) "If you choose to fight the tyrannical ruler for the single purpose of removing that vile ruler in the hope of liberating the people of land, then, that is one form of love indeed. Then there is the other kind of love, Woman, which I desperately, terribly seek you to understand my mind. For, Woman, when Lover seeks to fight tyranny in order for the purpose of liberating his particular Love of his life, then that, I tell you in all earnestness then that too is also a noble form and sacred type of Love. Do you find my words sensible?"

W: (Bored) "And, pray, if you wish to please my sensibility, how does your Lover know that he knows his Lover? Wherefrom does he get that certainty?"

M: (Excited & Speaking Rapidly) "He has that knowledge from Love itself! The energy of Love itself informs the Lover who to 'love' - and what he or she must do in order to achieve union with the chosen opposite lover. You see how blessed and powerful Love is for us mere mortals? It is an intelligent form of energy, Lady, think of my words. How do atoms know where to go and what to do? They just 'know'. Maybe, 'tis God that tells them. Here too, I speak to you, perchance God directs this exemplary 'Energy' called Love, to inform Lover to approach his or her Lover and that is why they fight injustice, sacrifice, and bleed tears of blood, till they truly one day, some day, join in flesh and mind!"

W: "And what of the changes that Man and Woman do undergo – how does Lover continue to relate to his or her opposite?"

M: "Again, for your beautiful question, I tell you this: only for the Lover who has been blessed with Love from our Lord Himself, then, no matter what changes exist within his opposite, the Lover will still, and for eternity love his Woman! That is the meaning of Love, Woman! You ask me, what is the definition of Love? I answer you truly, that is the meaning: that I, your Lover, will fight liars, and jesters, and hypocrites, and cruel deceivers for Your Sacred Cause and – hear me here – and even if you should die, the Man who loves, will fight still and forever even after your expiration! Never, ever to capitulate! Do you feel the boiling energy of furious rage that will not and never, ever accept the rule of the hypocrites and oppressors who oppressed my Lover?"

W: "What is your meaning of 'Sacred Cause'?"

M: "You missed a crucial vital, life producing word: 'Your'."

W: (Puzzled) "'Your' - And what?"

M: "Woman of Endless Beauties! The Sacred Cause can mean nothing when in the absence of the word 'Your'. So, listen now: the Lover will fight unto brutal, painful death, only for Your Sacred Cause. That Sacred Cause is for your Lover to do for eternity to fight for your, and only for your dignity, and only for your liberation, and only for your freedom, and only for your joy, and only for your prosperity, and only for your joy. The 'Sacred Cause' speaks to me who the Lovers love. And 'Your Sacred Cause' means your Lover will fight forever in order to give unto you and only you, your joy, your mirth, your pleasure, your comfort and all the beauties of our miserable existence."

W: (Bored) "But why take unto your already sun-drenched, parched and burdened body all these arduous tasks?"

M: (Surprised) "What? You still do not comprehend nor words, nor ideas and nothing for all that matters?!"

W: "No, unto you is to be an answer that needs be forthcoming. Speak for me, why should we beasts undertake all these blood-drenched battles and all for the attainment of the 'Love' of a Woman?"

M: "For sure! Indeed! That is a the beauty and reality and the truth of Love, for just as Life itself a never ending life and death struggle for existence, so too, is then, Love, for to attain Love, Man and Woman, or 'beasts' as you choose to call us, must necessarily and seek to ceaselessly struggle against death, and gloom, and despair to possess that holy union between flesh and mind between Man and Woman."

(Silence)

M: "To me, I believe that you feel Union is not that so necessary for Man and Woman?"

W: (Surprised) "On the precise opposite! Union is a need of all beasts, for it is a fundamental instinct within our starving bosoms. But your definition of what that 'Union' is meant to be, differs from your vision."

(Silence)

W: "Love is the Union of mind and flesh. That we all agree upon."

M: "Indeed."

W: "But in my planet, beasts, Man and Woman, ever change in their visions and in their feelings and in their needs and in their appetites and in their desires so that what Man originally 'loved' is no longer the same Woman that he once did love. And so how can you 'love' that which has utterly and completely altered into another being. That is truly a contradiction that defines nonsense; so, now – what say you?"

M: (Baffled): "Well, even though we do change with time, experiences and events and the effects of powerful memories, real Love will simply overcome all these difficulties and soon Flesh will reroute its way back to its Lover's Flesh and Mind will re-unite with his Lover's Mind. And should the two humans fail to reunite then all that can be said is that it was never Sacred Love in the first place."

W: "Yes, Man, but why crucify yourself for that Union? Union can be achieved through much easier means and paths."

M: (Shocked) "Why do you underrate the power of the eternal Union?"

W: (Laughing) "I've answered you already, dear Man. For what you so call 'Love' and 'Sacred' and 'Union' are all true to me – but they can all be achieved by much simpler ways than from your tortuous journeys – and you describe the struggle to achieve Union of flesh and mind as being like a life and death struggle. Well, listen to me, ye mortal Man, for you have overburdened yourself when I assuredly tell you, there are easier paths."

(Pause)

W: "Maybe not as intense, pleasure-wise, as your struggles, but as for the truth that God has allowed us only a brief moment in life wherein we are breathing, I can say this much: it is much better to follow the path I have chosen."

M: "But did you not before, unto may speak, telling me that your path for the Sacred Union of Flesh and Mind was exceedingly more pleasurable?"

W: "Conversing is the need to be as the tide. I can tell you this much: pleasure and its ferocious, unyielding intensities can only be experienced and defined by the receiver and so – unto you I say, perchance yours are weightier than mine."

M: "And so now what, Fair Lady?"

W: "And for now, either dream on or think on - in the paths you shall have to necessarily endure."

M: "And then?"

W: "Senseless questions requires of me none to be replied to."

M: (Confused) "I ask thee, do we be on this fiery planet, for the sake of sufferance only?"

W: "Yes, and no. I tell you that what is 'north' is unto thee, is true. Is it not. You see 'north' is the direction that only you and your constituents see, and, perhaps we ought to all applaud you and pat you and concede that you do indeed see the 'north' direction. But, then, for another creature, who sees from a southern angle, they will speak unto us, 'By Christ, we say, we see naught but a southerly direction!' Do we then disregard them?"

(Pause)

M: "So who speaks Truth then?"

W: (Patiently) "Both do, Man. For the creature who is from the northern angle, then what he does see, is a northern angle, and so for him, the 'north' is 'his' truth. And, as for the creature who locates himself in the southern location, then as for himself, his vision can only speak to him truthfully, that their vision is a southerly directed vision."

M: "So Truth has and have contradictory dualities that mutually oppose each other, and yet at the same moment, co-exist?"

W: "Correct, Man, for perhaps, you do now see some burning light, amidst this fiery blackness of this dead night of blackness?"

FINIS

CIRCUS OF LIFE!

An eyeless Monk confidently preached of the intricate complexities of the
Visions of Reality that he read somewhere;

The proud and haughty whore wept tears for
The literature she wrote
To illiterate moronic and strangely self-satisfied humans with lots of greedy gold coins;

Another sorrowful dove was harpooned yesterday, I felt
And I did dream of a boy awaiting to be gently impaled
Strange days, while the retarded games of fortune continue
To be churned out by the venerable
Institution of the Television industry
Confusing all well-wishers beyond politeness and exasperation
Still, someone shouts:
"Who can decide when the games shall cease?"

So, anticipation is in the murky, deathly air
As you wait to see her death, while she anxiously awaits her final exit;
Some hour later, they raise her to the questioning skies,
All watch in predictable belief and horror unheard of
Downwards she is released, flying fiercely towards a box filled
Yet, we never knew what it was filled with, so strange to relate;
She bounced from the huge box back into the air saddened
Till sweet, merciful death overtakes her
And all announcers analyse peacefully that all is at an end.

You know, I wondered what her crime was
To be worthy of such a tortuous death?
And this earth of yours somehow revolved still without excessively
Being repulsed by what happened
Tell the teenagers their pregnancies are burdens they cannot yet grasp

Those dying on the avenues of glamour and wealth
You have all wasted your minds and lives;
And the politician painted himself with silly images and visions
Both schizophrenic and empty
And insisted on speaking to yawning masses.

And still
There are humans who are faintly surprised
At our earthly life
That is decaying our stench infested souls
Do not ignore the Sad of the Earth

Do not ignore the Punished of the Earth

I warmly tell you.

CONFESSIONS OF A PROFESSIONAL
IDIOT – [MYSELF]

I have repeated myself
A million times
Imagine
Explaining my squalid behaviour
And humans did understand me
And, of course
I never realized
That everyone,
Yes, everyone
Understood my Self;
But, I myself never did
Understand my own Self
Throughout my existence
And
That, in itself, was
Yet another
Unbelievably
Idiotic
Grand Folly of mine;
And, of course,
Not surprisingly,
I never did even 'understand'

That truth

DEATH OF A CANDLE

The Candles' eye
That tries to express
Her passions' needs
While you all scream
Threatening to wilfully
Murder her

Beautiful Candle!
Trying not to
Flicker
Into an eternal extinction

I ask you all
Now
People of this life
How Hard can you
All become?

Warm essences and vehement smiles
Facing human steel
Co-imagining somehow
In between this confused air
Breathing and escaping

Angel Candle
Why humans seek your extinction
I do not understand
For what crime have you done
Save to enlighten men, women and children?

Your life
I tell you

Is ending.

Distant Wisdom

1. For those who question

What words are meaningful to them

Those who need

Questions whose origins are practical to them

Yet, do not suffer sorrow, nor despair

Life's pauses, you must accept

For the vision in the distance remains

Awaiting thee

An oasis, real and final.

2. When some ask you of errors

Of indignities, of sadness

Do not turn inside

In search of answers

Answers of pain, answers of futility

Do not burn yourself

Your one heart beating

Stillness defined much wisdom

Stillness, the twin sister of Patience was wisdom's bride

Yes, many suffer

Many grieve

Of itching and flagrant wounds

Of obscene and frightful deformities

Of faces you no longer recognize

Yes, many are chained

Their limits are defined

Bear the hatreds within your chest

Restrain the deeds for the proper hour

Otherwise, spent you shall be

Spent, as the lost leaf falling

Guided by the whims of an uncaring wind

Think, then, of where you shall fall

Think, then, of how hard you would fall.

3. The shambles of History

The follies of conversations

The dullness of so many minds

Breathe this air you breathe

Contemplate the thousands of those before you

For, you are not alone

What you undergo has been repeated

Repeated in the self-same shambles of History

History!

History is the history of Man

The history of You

From dictators and their pawns

To yawning democracies

Whose subjects are equally dead

How then, do people ignore it?

When a soldier suffered of thirst choking in some century

And another soldier suffered the same in another century

Where does the difference lie?

4. In your life, you recognize repetitiveness

Recognize, then, history's repetitiveness

Understand therefrom

And what do you say to the one who cares not for hope?

For those forced on the streets of wilderness and decay

What do you say to those whose culture is vice?

Distant as you are

Or, close as you are to them

Or one them you may be

What words do you say?

The spark must arrive

The spark for organized movement

One that involves them

That is for their guidance

Therefore, unto the streets you too must journey

Unto the streets of decay and into their hearts

Say a world of vast superiority can exist

A different world

A world of harmony can be

That is all

To feel that thought is the key

For, few believe it

Few care

Soul's forgotten

Themselves, they forgot!

Themselves, they killed!

In life's myriads

In life's experiences

And varied and incomprehensible emotions

In life's sudden dullness

The shocks

Take heed

Understand the oceanic ignorance that exists

Understand your enemies

Understand the existence of fools and idiots

The existence of human insects

Understand the existence of torturers who smile genuinely

Of poets, who understand little

Understand the existence of the varieties of human beings

Then, you shall never allow your heart

To hear the words and feelings of surprise

Understand the depths of those who stand before you yesterday, today and tomorrow.

Understand their cravings

Understand their real intentions, motivations and desires

These are the humans

Of which, you may be one
For every human seeks your Anguish

5. Sigh carefully, then

Sigh understandingly, what battalions you face

Understand the nature of the hidden gunfire aimed at you

Understand the decoys aplenty

Within that context, exist to expand justice and permanent equality

Exist, to help the lonely

Exist, to help the pained one

The crying one

The sufferers; the chained; the blinded

The deafened; the mutilated; the abused;

The raped; the beaten; the ignored one

Souls forgotten

Soldiers unknown

What path did they take?

What passions did they have?

What thoughts crossed their minds?

Souls forgotten

Throughout this world

Suffering in silence

Suffering in loneliness

Who will touch them?

Who will shelter them?

Where are you all tonight?

Ye ghosts from the deeds of idiotic, uncaring humans

Who decided on your fatal fates?

When?

And for whom did you once cheer

When your existence was being decided upon?

6. Souls forgotten!

I tell you, you are no different than forgotten soldiers

All have been trampled upon

All have been abused

Daily and hourly

And in their remembrance,

And in your to-be remembrance

You shall all be forgotten!

As the unknown martyred soldiers have been forgotten

Forgotten by the dust of their remains

By skulls deliberately fractured

By the scattered limbs

Truths do exist

Yet, truth's greatest enemy

Is Ignorance.

DON'T WORRY IF YOU SHOULD SEE ME

And if normality were to come back to me
So suddenly
A beauty to be
In my real life
To help me
Can that really be?
Because
I have become rather
Brittle
Didn't you know?
Now you ought to know
Friends of mine
That I no longer really know
Any of you;
The sadness
In my years
And in the sick oceans of my life
Have been
Far too exhausting
So, don't you worry too much
If you should see me
It may all come back to me
After all, I've lost it all through my own
Mismanagement
No?

ESSENCES I FEEL

Hearing

Smiles lasting

Times twisting

In aches

Painful

Turning mindless

Away, you're away

Travels involuntary

To where?

To where?

A scream I've felt

Scream that frightened me

Widespread panic

Humanity hurting

Poverty unjust

What are you hearing?

In us

A community

Community of ethics

We're flying

Far, far away

You're all far, far away

Help me

Gather closer

Where I can feel

Where I can touch

Turn these screams melodious

In moments euphoric

I see horizons of serious and joyous Art

Where I see passions turned eternal true

Turn a hand to me

The essences I feel

I swear this life

Can be so much more

This life can be so much more.

FUGITIVE FROM INJUSTICE

Welcome me into your Life!
Welcome me into your Mind
The one
That rejected my angry Life
And her repressed Soul;
Will you welcome me then
Today?
Because -
Because it is so cold
This strange dawn of yours,
It burns with a freezing
Hatred
Lashing out at my terrified smile
That will try
And try still
To exist
In this bewildering World
Of yours.
Welcome me, then, please
In this arctic climate of yours
Where polite protocol
Means more than poverty's needs
Where irrelevant conversations
Mean more than starving anxieties
Please!
Welcome me
Somewhere
Because you see
In truth, I can no longer
Run from you;
By now I am trying to run
From my own breaking Self
That, yes, has so much
Failed me
In this your
Planet of Freezing Lives.

GALA AWARDS FOR PEDOPHILES

And many times
I did, hope
Many times, I've meant to speak
But where exactly is the use of it all?
For 'use' was far – too far away
While uselessness killed me here
I tried to expand my mind
To meet the beginnings of love
But how useless
I screamed
Everyone's a criminal in his
And her
Own way
And you know that yourself
This, then, is the existence of the meandering river
Somehow we find ourselves
Within it all
Within the parties and conferences and meetings
Of social criminals
And gatherings of women beaters
And charities for child abusers
We've got to smile
Shake hands and act sincere!

GIVE UP GIVING

Come to give
And you'll live
This life
From an
Uncertain trial
Of sarcastic jurors
Whose only concern
Are painful recollections
Scattered by
Hungry, vengeful
Lovers
So, give up giving
My soul
And live life

Therefrom.

GOD – PLEASE GIVE ME PEACE?

1. I am deaf as a door knob
Blind as darkness
And mute as a pebble
I am disabled by persecuted luck
Wherever I go
And whatever I try to do
I break down

2. I know really well
What constitutes myself
Are fragmentary entities
Hating each other
And that makes me
Crippled in my mind
And in my behaviour
I hope you are understanding
My words and their heat?

3. I wake each morning feeling happy
And then
That first flicker of madness
Really hits me
Telling me
This new day
Will be like
All your yesterdays
And then, I ask myself
'What am I to do with my life?'

4. I have two choices
Either to go and suffer your torture
Or I end my sickening life
And I see myself continuing
In this 'Life' that is Hell for me
I do not need people
I do not need friends

I do not need family
For, you see, I have none
I never did have any
And before you feel 'pity' for me
Let me tell you quickly
I have no 'need' for family
Friends, lovers or any humans

5. I cannot go outside my house
The house I do not even own by the way
Anyway, I cannot go outside
Why?
Because I have yet another disease
Fear of the vast expanses of space
How idiotic it sounds to you, I do know
But there you go, I've got that damned disease
As well
And so I must remain at my home, inside

6. Because
We are the *Sick*
That is what God has wished for us
We are isolated
Because we embarrass you
And I am embarrassed to be with you
Normal souls
That is why we have to be isolated
There's Logic even in Madness!

7. 'Who' can help me?
No one
Is there any medications for my brain?
No there are no medications for my brain.
Why is it that no one helps me?
Because no one can help me
So I am alone to face the Panic
On my own

8. What is this 'fear' I keep talking about?
I don't want to talk about it
Actually it is because I cannot talk about it
Because
Whenever I talk about it
I feel the Panic will return against my mind

9. How can I communicate with you?
We are so far apart

And, to be truthful
You are so lucky not to understand or feel
What I have to go through ever day in
My sick life
Christ, I wish I could live your life!

10. When I am in my car
And we are driving towards the highway
This fear is beyond words
I need, I feel, I have to smash my forehead
Against the window door
To create severe blood
In order to 'stop' the
Threat of Panic from bubbling
Into a Reality

11. When I was in a train, once
The Threat of Panic bubbled in myself
I felt the only way to
Extinguish that F.E.A.R. was to
Open the door of the running train
And for me to throw myself out
From my seat and onto
The moving rail tracks
And thereby my Death
Would end the agonising Torture
The emanates from
The 'mere' Threat of Panic
Through my Death

12. I am talking of the mere
'Threat of Panic'
Imagine how frightening that is
And imagine what a real, full blown Panic
Attack would do to me?
Christ, how am I to function in this life
That you, my Lord, gave me?
Or, perhaps, you are insinuating that
I should sever the arteries of my Life?

13. These are my serrated words
These are my jagged words
What do I mean by 'Ravaged Words'?
I mean I have been shredded through
Splintered, battered by my own
Uneasy, sick brain
That is fanatically determined to
Nail me at every second that I dare to
Breathe
Why?
Why, my God?
You chose that I have to be
Slaughtered and bruised
Way beyond belief
Or, way beyond human belief
Can comprehend

HOW CAN I UNDERSTAND THAT WHICH IS UNDEFINABLE?

Girl is lost again and is that a crime?
But for you, it is a 'crime'
And so you scream at her abuse and verbal excrement

Colours of emotions are confusing
Which one is which
Which is sincere and which is not
Touches deep
In sensitivities
While others equally
Hurt, debasing you

Where are you going?
What to where?
Who's to where?
And the same old random romances repeat themselves
Ad infinitum
As jolly drinks become dry
And initial sparkles cease to be anymore

Lost girl
Seeking silky winds
And friendly eyes
And profound hope
Distant
That is what I see
Distances far too expansive
Far beyond your reach

Hunger
Shining fists
Glowing against you
What can you believe in
When will sorrows cease
When will daybreaks proclaim
Serenity and peace and defiance eternal

You'll understand
What we feel
Elevated and serene
Dreaming passionately
Harmonies can be
Love can be
For the evolving girl-child
Begging through her smashed tears
To the innocent imprisoned ones
Asking for an answer
Within us all can be
Within us all can be

How Come No One Noticed The Killers of Jesus?

He spoke of love

Breathed, dreamed love

Infused and

Exuded Love
Loved all of us and also
For Humanity and her evil ways;
Lord Jesus; butchered in the
Name of the Love of the Kiss
Of Hypocrisy -
The Hypocrisy
That Man finds
So natural

Gentle soul!
Betrayed by the Greatest of your Followers
Betrayed by them, that so adored and
Them, that so night and day venerated
You the most
Betrayed by them, those whose
Worshipped you day and night

Strange imprints!
Did you people notice?
Imprints were deliberately
Planted everywhere and in front of our paths that we
Daily trod upon
How was it we did not understand and feel
What venality was silently mumbling against us
Silently, but with dead seriousness in their intentions
To execute their plans of butchery

And who were these creators of psychotic malevolence
Creators of clues and imprints and
Suggestive seductive whispers?
Do you not stop to think
In your materialistic, phony, plastic,
Under nourishing lives that it was none other
Than them, the same adoring crowds?
Yes, they were, after all, the same venerable
The Founding Brothers and Sisters
Who were your determined killers
Of Him that they
Night and day
Venerated
As a Spokesman for our Lord God

It was themselves, you knew and talked to
Who so casually replaced the truths
With the simplest and most digestible sugary falsities
And why did not your Disciples
Seriously notice these clues of the evil intentions
That were so abruptly to be
His sickening Reality
Committed with such real love
Against our and Your Beloved Son?

I declared to no one
Out there
In my imagined audience
My presumed people
You see

Endless deaths
Are coming
Now
Through the reels of our news
And nothing was ever surviving
The bloody blasts from the merrily drunken revolutionaries
Who are killing now
For killing's sake
And so let's laugh out this unending holocaust night
Out

No one really understands this
System that we once create in our ancient past
Listen, here!
A charming serial killer
Philosophised about the differing values
Of existence
And in the end
Yes, he
Managed to don the ugly and deformed clown's killer mask
And entertain all you approving fools
Out there
you did laugh
And enjoy
This squalid situation

HOWLS OF AN INSANE WOMAN

1. A vague impression wept
Dews of insecure passion
Small passions founded on severe fear
Unheard of

2. Another beauty dies
Here and now
As we think and as we read now
Another dying suffering one
Suffocates now
From another grotesque grasp
Of Humanity

3. And these ones will not fade away
Their corners coming closer
As their sorrows exponentially expand
So weep no more
My face dries
For none can actually hear us here

4. O vague impressions!
The wilderness and loneliness
Is our home
Our forced home
Unheard and unseen personalities
We are, we think
Do you really think you can fly anywhere?

5. A staggering heart once wrote poetry
Unguided words
Words from a fragmented, severely
Sliced up heart
An unknowing heart
Did you scream at the sorrows you daily see
The hardships you daily suffer
The opportunities weep

Savoir! Saviour!
Save our lives!
Here and now

6. This meaninglessness is killing us all!
I scream!
Far too profoundly
Here is our now and our today
This is our 'now'
Not tomorrow
And not our yesterdays
It's our 'Now's' that we need
You saviours out there!

7. There was Hunger and a hating Smile
Youth turned away wearily
The candles of love wept
Melting breaths
A scream rings in me
With no hope of escape
A beauty
Whose life parallels my life

8. Suffering
Believing she has convictions
But she never really knew herself
But the screams reverberated endlessly
While the babies
Of my mind shrieked.

****

HUMANS ARE HURTFUL CRUMBS

Hopeful last breaths
Death's final instincts
Receding from you;
When will we accept
The meek have gone?
When will we eye the final mountaintop?

Truths weeping, as the end nears
As honesty lies crippled, beaten and bruised beyond repair
And the pulverized human dust can no longer speak
How can we ever
Allow ourselves to be so abused?

Tell me, then of your spiritually desolate sighs
Tell me, of the horrors minute by minute
How will I stand on that day
As my life on your earth dies of grief wrenching?

For the Humiliated
For the Degraded
For the Ashamed
You
In context, understand your enemies
In context, measure the moments foul
The days foul
Measure the Contexts of Grief
The ills that occur may be your doings.

Others are unjust, I know
But try to understand that 'justice' is abstract:
I tell you sincerely,
Humans do not feel justice
And so justice is meaningless.

Understand humans because
By understanding them
You then know what to do;
Understand the worthlessness of your Savage Species
Understand that humans are mostly
Hurtful Crumbs from the Devil's faeces;
Only then will you seek fulfilment
And, also comprehension
Of what your Life is.

I KNOW I'M KILLING MYSELF

I try here
This life
To restart
Bread
I dream of
That warm bed
I need
But is not mine
And I turn away
From them all
Because within me
Is an unknown disease
Naturally enough
It betrays my sanity

This beautiful food here
That is not for me
I stand here and nowhere
Unaware of the dangers
The mistakes I do
Are piling up
And these years of mine
Are telling me
That my trials of tearful
Pain
Will eventually

Murder my soul.

Lady of the Secluded Ponds

Eyeless flower
In minds of unrest
Sing this melody in warmth abundant.

Troubled Skies have chosen
To forsake you
While you crowds seek to intermingle
With lovers un-affected
Do you yet again fail to comprehend?

Moon-less sky
Come and perchance you may
Yearn in me, to visualise
A show of Truth
That dances
The Dance of Closure

And yes what cried – cried!
That is my understanding
Of History
Where outbreaks of madness
Virulently burst out
Far too often
In uncontrollable rages;

Gentle lady!
In the midst of it all;
Come to feel
That your
Flowers in your mouth
Will bring bitterness
And not deliverance
For that which is
Constitutionally brittle
Cannot last

Think, then
Think!
Soft Lady
Of Ponds Warmly
Enclosed.

LETTER FOUND ON DEAD WOMAN

O Sweetness
And if life
So now
Still fails me
I guess
I'll so surrender then
To this
My lost
Smile
And her only hurt secret
That so affected my grief

This, then
Was my beginning
In a world, my world
Of such an expanding sorrow

And so Goodnight
Sweetness
Of my
Own life
That forever allowed me
Her serious pleasures
Whist so denying me
Clearness of Mind
Goodnight.

LIFE'S CONCRETE KNOWLEDGE

Some spoke, some cried, some threatened lives by words

A dawn's dawning yawning gradually for hope

Progress unsure...the crowds threatened to know

To bleed and to ulcerate for crumbs of words

Blinding and to thrust waves ferocious

Onto souls drowning and insecure by life's concrete

Knowledge that was stabbed by wealth

Shaken by demons of luxury and rotten frontiers

Twisted by unemotional, greedy creatures unalive

Crowds burning just to feel, to rage, to burst

To tear open these wings

To thunder passions across the Heavens ripped so meekly apart

Crowds so expecting the fire...the crowning, triumphing speeches

Expecting the grand gestures, artistic and fulsome

Fulminating towards kings parasitical and stuffed vermin

Guillotined labour drenched rivers and oceans

To scream forth and to be alive in haste.

MY BABY BOY, PIDI

Sweet son
My beautiful baby boy!
My angel baby
I see enemies supporting you
Their kisses are stabs
Their love is poison
Screaming to discard you
Beautiful boy
Pidi!
Understand my attempts
To gather truths
From a stolen basket of mainly stupidities
And when I lie down
I see angels
In my bed
And while I survive
I live through the Devil's mercy
How odd!
How odd!
I adopted two gorgeous girls
And I did love them
In eternity
But they were not able
To realize
My thoughts
For them
At all.

MY BELOVED SON

Sweet child

And if I did regret my life

Will you understand

These mistakes

And endless errors

Coming over me

Beloved son

Forgive me

My faults

For I have not sinned

In this life.

MY EXIT THAT I COULDN'T FIND

And yes, if my life
Was so to be
An ending dilemma
That I couldn't
Solve
Then shouldn't I be looking for
An Exit for myself?

Gentle souls
Listen to my emotions
Just as I then again
Tried to escape and fail

My own
Heartbreaking rain
This that pours
And seethes
So continually
Upon my invisible raw Mind
Leaving me unable to push on and ahead

This I can't understand;
My Exit
Unto Happiness
I could never find -
Therein was my
Simple Sorrow.

REJOICE!

May joy cure all heartaches

May the chants, parades and tears

Burst your soul with fire alive

May the seeds of glory and martyrdom

Spring forth from the poundings of tyranny

May the countless weeping's and sorrows cease

For so at last

A direction-laden spirited wind harks

Oh! Awaken to the light –

Your chains melt now

And your faces glow with joyfulness

Never again to suffer...

Never again to agonize...

The moment sweeps the idle

And the mocking flee past their insignificance

Laugh and rejoice all ye people

Rejoice!

SAD WOMAN

While she drank
Her crusty eyes
Begging, aching to be needed
Her blue elbow
Sang tortured truths.

What we saw
Was too much
Before we dried our hearts
From a beginning
That just cried
To end now.

And she wept her needs out
Strangling words
From a dry, flaky, ragged skin;
So drink your empty drink
Till you can see
No longer
In this ending distant night
Of a coldness that cried
From your tired beliefs.

Staggering that early morning
Where someone just had to
Pick you up
From your oblivion
Sweet woman
Your crutches have withered
So long ago.

SAVAGE IS LIFE

A question in me

Where senses dance

Tunes insane

Where imaginations

Caress skies heaving

Uncertain winds

Carrying fate

Of ours here

Sweetness, I seek

An image serene

A protector long dead

Where compassion

Is beingness

Where truth

Is passion

Within us

Tell the forgotten

Tell the despairing

Children of sorrow

Young and old

Savage is life

Savage it is!

SO NEAR, YET SO FAR

Upon whom is the Passage
Safe?
The Passage of Life
Trapped
You stand insecure
Unsure, fearful
Within the nearness
Of truth
You are
And yet,
Stranded, startled
Frozen
You cry?

SUDDEN SUICIDE

Eyeless mask
Ugly night
Going somewhere
She thought
Sudden knife
You pose
At your nerve
Killing madness
And ending
All discourse

TALKING TO A SUICIDAL WOMAN

Too good?
My truths and needs are being
Remanufactured
By recluses
Who were smiling
In front of fake mirrors
Produced by self deceiving professional liars

'What can I do with you?' I asked you so many times
But you always gave me such
Twisted answers
With the logic of Satan
You thought
My rationality was being coy
But it wasn't, my dearest
It was just my absurdities

And yet
We had all to live
Within these
Claustrophobic days
And pointless heated discussions
With their excessive baggage of tears
And rages
That duly achieved a naught

I saw nothing but more of my depressions
That seemed like snarling waves too me
Seriously trying to murder myself
Coming and going
But always returning
And maybe succeeding soon with myself?

THE ADVICE OF A SAGE WOMAN

A woman came

From Nowhere to speak

To Men.

"I speak of colours aplenty

Have I tempted thee?

Your scattered ears laugh at me

Your directionless wind whistles in unruly anger

So listen to me, my children

Think not I have come to tempt you

Listen hard to me

For your sufferings

I tell you

Shall not cease

I am so sorry

For I have no better words for your lives

You have perhaps seen the unread pages of History

These stories are being played out today

In your very own lives

On your soil that you tread on

Repetition is the essence of History

And all will truly be forgotten

Your blindness will condemn your sad Destiny fast!"

Then, the Woman wept and begged to be heard

While the learned Men walked on

In paths they knew nothing of.

THE ANONYMOUS LETTER SIGNED 'SARAH'

The death of a stranger
Who once cried in the streets of cold
And yet wrote words of hope

As I ached for a spiritual sleep
Wherein such cruel mornings awakened us all
The meanings of my passions were lost
Their motives became unknown to me

While the crowds gathered their lives
In processions dictated
At a predetermined hour
They gathered to sing futile prayers
As the storms of boredom swept the anxious ones
Their passions
Were masked forever more

- Sarah

THE BARREN SKULLS

April 26, 1989 – Boston

A chance unexpected

The door closed

Unseen opportunity

Darling woman

Life's statues that I see

I'm hearing fading music

Look on

Look ahead

The winds will twist soon

Their paths never understood

No day

No day is the same

They tell me

And tomorrow will present you with new events

I can't believe too much

Preach to the donkeys

Ugly beasts of burden

Feel the sorrow for the suffocated and ignored

And who looks at who?

In this planet here

Planet revolving

And my life is stationary, I swear

So the chances come in like coincidences

Whilst the dancer explained her motions

To senile judges

Sensuality embraced the barren skulls that preside over us

How fair, my God

Time and again

The night wanderer prayer for water

The deserts howled in windy laughter

And another dancer reeked with sorrow

Dance of the sand storms

Poor souls, poor families

What you're needing

It's all so fading

What you desire

It's all been stolen years ago

Your gods, your idols

Seek revenge against them

Only then will your journeys and sensualities

Have meaning.

THE EMPTY HUMAN

All your conversations, they can go on
For all the time, that one can listen
Hearing words of the Master and the Slave
How could you continue this lie of living loneliness?
In your empty mansions
The truths are all waiting for you
And you continue
In your diary of professional nothingness
But, you hurt!
The only one who can tell you
And judge you so truly within
The emptiness
Has himself
Dried out.

Civilization!
I tell you, your perception of your own Self-Worth
Has long been dying from neglect pure;
Your soul needs Emotional Depths and Substance
And not the masked saviour you loved yesterday;
Your scattered Soul needs
Substance from words, gestures and promises
And you must no longer peep at the liar's glances
That felt free
To dance
In any motion and movement it felt;
While you stood there, consuming nothing from your insecure saviour –
You stand there alone,
Drenched by brittle dryness and desperately waiting for an unknown appointment
In a hidden destination in No Man's Land;
You stand there still waiting
Waiting for your hero's suggestions;

While your passions that explode so discretely
You then realize just how much you need
Your own Emotional Essences
Your Emotional Essence needs the bleeding to stop
Now
As you attempt to amputate your soul's troubled edges.

For all your friendless 'friends'
And their posh gatherings
And the glamorous wicked nights
Where money was nonsense
In the eyes of your Self
You still stand there alone
Thinking of the moments
Of so many years ago
Viewing your life's scenery
That you so feel for
All troubling
And adding to nothing
Nothing and going fast nowhere
Speaking words, feelings and ideas
Arguing and loving and working
Dressing your body -
But, whatever you may do
Strips you bare ever more
Strips you your scant and remote truths
That are dwindling;
Starving in your empty civilization
That is descending into a
Frozen death!

THE FINAL POEM MAN WILL WRITE

Come then, to write your words
They, that filled
And inspired
So few

For before you
Were grounded
So many songs
Of truths
Forgotten

And now you
Write what beliefs
Exist within you
But I say this:
Folly of your minds
Shall be
The Final Poem
Man will Write.

THE GREAT PRETENDER!

I was never too sure
If I was right or wrong
They were just mere abstractions to me
My mind of nothingness you wish to visit?
I loved this one
Or that one
What did I know
About all of them, I knew nothing
That was my truth
But, then, I didn't know my truths
Nor did they!
I lived roles
I breathed images
I continued to produce
Manufactured thoughts
Manufactured opinions
That I then
Believed were
To be truths
And then guess what
I defended these manufactured stones
And I became passionate
For them;
Idiot soul!
How can stones
Be passionate?
I dressed this way and more
And did talk in this style
But what was it all to mean

I thought
It meant so much!
But it meant naught really
I was a nothingness real
Living in a vivid world
Of vaguest abstractions
Wherein the end
Emptiness
Was the grand net total
Created between us all here, for now..
I went to universities
To study the philosophy of stupidities
Yes, my God, indeed!
How I never even managed to learn that much
These philosophies
Of Nothingnesses!

THE INHUMAN JOURNEY

Peace; Souls, herewith are the Blessings of Certainty
Passed unto the Needy
Across agitated oceans of distances
Never part with your beliefs

Peace, Souls migrating, from lands Harsh to lands Unknown
There may be no relief in this world
Yet, tomorrow, in the skies there shall be Serenity Supreme
Press ahead, then; press ahead, in your Inhuman Journey

THE PARANOID LOGICIAN

I'm beginning
In my
Mind
To *believe*
In a
Truth;
But Truth
Abandons me -
And so
I exist
Mindless
And alone.

THE SPRIT SHALL LIVE

Sweetness

For if life

Were to be

Hard

Come to live

Then

In this mindless time

Where brothers

Are locked

In so much

Hatred

Where the oceans

Of anguish

Are so surprised by

Their own hopeless selves

Sweetness

This sudden need

Will die

And your spirit

Will live

Just as you

Shall forget

Me and my lives

Forever becoming

You shall be

A truth

In front of all

You deaf listeners!

THE TYRANT'S FINAL SPEECH

My dearest souls!
So far away placed
I tell you this
My mind to convey
The strange and the passionate
Perhaps you have seen me
This creature here
In a world so far away
Your thoughts of me
Do not surprise
Nor amaze my heart
What **you know of my mind**
I already knew
In a world of insecurity
Where none can be trusted
Nor loved
In a world of aching agonies
That may not be disclosed
Where you all fear none but yourselves
O such a World!
Such a desperation I can see
And none can face
Wedding their fears
Onto illusions
Strongly held
Never to cast themselves alone
Never to see their pale eyes
So disturbed and dry
My mind's pulses can feel
Hatred's beautiful sharpness
And if, as I must
Upon a thousand moments
Tear and pierce myself
And envision my **changing face**
These scars and their children's tears
Would you then understand?

My friends!
Do you not remember?
What **impulses can Rage**
Knocking on all perceived shames
And vices
This tired soul of mine
I must understand
Can't you see
What emptiness can create?
The pressures within Me I have to control
And never to publicly show?
What these lethal Passions can destroy
Rendering you miserable and alone
In an ended struggle so unromantic and vile.
And yet!
There is Freedom
Freedom from fear's spasms
That can Only be felt by You
And, if extreme conviction was my shield
Perhaps, my friends, perhaps
And, if hatred was really obscene
Maybe...maybe
For what I can do
And have done
Will be applauded by you someday
When in the quieter hours
You, too, shall plunge into my world
As detrimental and sarcastic as it may be
You, too, will lose your vision.
My friends! My real friends!
So far apart we may be
Listen, then, to these words I create
My Mask - I did make
My Destiny - I did create
But, remember that I am but Mortal
Human, *fallible* and true

And, if driven and committed I am
Moulding a thousand deeds and lives
Wonder for once
Where from come the Seeds for these
My friend!
I am but one of labour's ranks
And martyred by capital and greed;
No services served me
No goods, nor Gods could I believe in
So I can only replace with all that stood
Against me;
My path, I laid out before me -
The lines, I arranged and defined
Between the sane and insane;
O these wars I waged
Were only a shot in the dark!
And now
These words so clear I write
In moments now passed
I have become one of history's treasures
Adorned or rotting
My life's conquests dismissed
My existence betrayed
So reason with me now
For life can only be so much lived
And destroyed.

UNKNOWN SOLDIER

You tried to whisper words in a scream

That all came forth far too convoluted

Doom's clouds raining fierce

Against the luxuries of those who dream

This is indeed
A terror to gasp – A tale to tell
Of far too great dimensions

Oh! Emotional contradictions wearying supreme

You tried to cry; you tried to voice responsible ideas –

But you were met with pupils in trances aloud:

Entities too proud

To admit shame, defeat and grief

Entities to proud to weep.

Soul, laden with beauty, transformed into a reckless recluse –

With a gasping audience of universal fools

So drugged and self-abused

Tell me Why?

You didn't hear the news
On the stabbing of Jesus in His hour of gloom?
Do you think History has relevance to us all, or not?

Unknown Soldier!

Your tale, the careless winds have drifted them away;

And generations are none the Wiser, my dears

For all of our done pained deeds

We all turn away – for wherever a limp light may flicker

Unknown Soldier!

With a proud Mother and your bland, simple name

A childhood; a cosy love and a thousand memories more

Your treasures fell with you – secrets and all

Unknowing characters spoiled and tainted your pride

Providing you with even further Pain

While you gaze at this earth and her History
From your simple trenches
And it is all Passing by you

Oblivious

And carrying no shame nor any morality

Unknown Soldier!

Unknown as you are and unknown you shall for Eternity be:
Though they counsel you, "They Shall Not Be Forgotten!"

I do wonder, What minds taught you throughout your life?

From behind their tattered veils?

Unknown Soldier!

Unknown as you are –

Your pride pushes you to serve on

But, Should it, too, fall some moment,

I hope it Will never turn to dust

No! And a thousand years or more

May pass;

Throughout which, a million human clowns in wandering disgrace
Will live out their merry lives

Your Dignity remained;

Forever shall remain

A symbol, a painted canvas of colours, literature and music;

Forever a burden for all my lameness

Forever etched, carved and inscribed
In my brain

For masses to witness

Though you remained in your briefest of life forever tormented
By the most insignificant

Haunted by the smirking insane

Didn't they tempt your insecure strengths?

And threatened your fulsome stability aloud?

O Unknown forgotten fool and a bore

Collapsed in your once great might

And became such a forgotten wind of brevity;

Your mask, eternal, piercing and true;

Will sit there abused, sickly and aloof –

All can and will laugh again or more –

For you are no burden unto anyone

Your Existence, once so stubborn, is now speck of dust

For all the wicked masses who may wish to see:

And for what exactly?

For Ancient and Modern History?

Monument that you are –

You perished amidst the yawning spectators, my dead friend

Your physicality has long since been scattered
In its trivial remains
Amidst the condescending living ones

Across the ages

O! Unknown Soldier!

Having dispensed with your life's pleasures, worthy and real

So wretchedly

Agonizing, as you did

For so long a days;

Why despair and bury your Ugly Self now

So miserably?

Do you regret your service now?

As you review and witness your decades and years

Questioning what worth it contained therein

No! My man;

For treasures of any entity are not to be clung to and kept

And this is my gentle wisdom unto you

May you now Translate it into a thousand languages and their feelings;

And by the grace of endurance, will and a knowledge
Of certainty
You may feel peace

For such is Victory Immortal

To be forever and eternally

True.

~

VILE 'HUMAN'

An evening wherein I find sitting
Supper's Traitor sitting gleeful next to me
And so Begins the eerie moment
That I feel
Seeks to wilfully extinguish
A life's fragile candle.

The incomprehensible scenes I see
In my silent eyes
Seemingly never ending
Wild expanses
Visions of Hurt, Sorrow and Loneliness
That I cannot understand, define or explain.

Seeking any role to play
We turned for comfort
To any random guiding and guided Fool
Look at the utter beauty of the liars
Around us all
Spelling mistakes they make, though we heard poetry
That seriously changed our brief lives.

But we mustn't lie about our mistakes
Let us listen to our deathly end's opening night
Coming so soon
A majestic Silence and Symphony
For all our final moments
To ponder about.

And are we still acting, we, the despised 'human'
Acting beyond reason and its compassion
My God
We shall soon meet you
And how will we then react?

Ancient victim,
Still writing
Your romantic scripts for senseless lovers
I will tell you
Do not accept or forgive the glamorous Remorse of Judas
Seek his annihilation, without a breath of mercy

Forsaken children,
Abandoned by the vilest parent creatures Man has known
Tears of your Farewell
That will soon be Forgotten
Are screaming still
So think just how
Awfully pointless they all are.

* * * *

WE ARE ALL PRISONORS IN THIS LIFE

Ruined, filthy room, despite your brave cleansing attempts
Messengers mentioned and whispered and hinted where the escape keys may be
Cautiously the feelings of prophets and the self proclaimed prophets
Preach their manuscripts on how to achieve freedom
Silently, I heard a shy, insecure tune that was meant to soothe your nerves
The crazed smiles of a common lunatic expressed momentary sincerity
Followed by the most rigid, faulty shallowness
While solemn, pompous psychiatrist men and woman insisted on continuing their talks
For no reasons that I personally understood
And we all wished them a speedy end
For they lavishly created uncertainties and fears
And lots of cash, too!

The terribly bored skies were beginning to randomly mock us
In everything between our insides hidden
The couple of bored lovers played
The prescribed game for them, again and again
Ad nauseam
While a severely overweight clown with
Mascara and greedy sweat heavily mingling
Suddenly begat to laugh so hysterically
At himself and at everyone else
Why, I really thought he was going fall from his feet.

Smoking cannot be good, twenty serious thinkers thought
And they thought really hard
At that proposition
Thinking that humans would be interested
To hear what thoughts they were thinking about
Yet, but when did anything – like thoughts or thinking - matter to bored humans?
You must have guessed some of the god's
Worthless tricks being played upon us!

And blessed are the sincere liars, for they do materially so well in life
Life that is presumed to be filled with truths, love, compassion and humanity
The innocent ones wept, for they were hurt you know by
Their blatant inability to act the required roles!
Now you must have felt humanity's pinch, I wondered for these hurt ones?
And to the astonishment of all:
Nobody really felt anything for the innocent ones.

The times spoke ancient tales for the ready-made and pre-packaged human beings
If you do believe in life so much, you may well die for its gruesome offensiveness
Crying for the blood of the blinded and handcuffed one who did naught
"Go die, I screamed in my wisdom forlorn, for we are all prisoners here!"

What use and benefits did the venerable senators and congressmen do for you all?
If you love the Mortuary Men,
Then what else can you expect from them?
Life! – Are you that stupid!?

The intense experiences you think of, were all fake
All the times you presumed were truthful, loving and passionate were insincere
Kill those memories of infectious trash, and they'll tell you soon
The roads of life are vaguely manifold, you must have known
So feel the Skin of your Soul, here and now;
And live for no other purpose
The ones who sigh, know it all.

The loving trees and their adoring branches were amputated yesterday
By conservationists seeking votes;
And yes, we dutifully applauded praised the times for its truths and sincerities
All the time, I was alone
Desperately trying to gather my Self, here and nowhere
Yet between it all, I swear my dysfunctional, distant heart did say so:
Saying scornful messages to me;
Within our wearied Soul, across the breathtaking boundaries of time and space
I felt I needed to laugh
As soon as I feel I am in the Heavenly Skies
The Skies we shall all so soon beautifully share in harmony pure!

WHAT DIFFERENCE DOES IT MAKE?

Waiting
And Time, remains waiting for you
Asking you to understand it
Sorrow's gowns have been disrobed
The figure of flesh expresses itself being naked
Some exist expecting to be embalmed
Others to be destroyed forever

Sad of the Earth!
I call upon thee all to awaken
And understand the meanings
Of your plight's trails
And your forgotten lives
For existence is struggle,
And it is a spiteful struggle
Within anger everywhere brooding, festering
In directions aimed at anyone

Kill the pompous
The oppressors
The self-pitying professional fools
Look at those idle mansions
And the casually squandered riches

And I see a new religion shall be heralded
That I do see
Passionate communalism ethical and warm, it shall all be
Where else can life wander to?
Ask yourselves these words unto your selves, I ask you
Hate the liars and the self-hating and the vain and the extravagant ones
See the colours of life scattered
Know the art of mixing colours
Know the art of juxtaposing colours
Know the art of ideas presented by the holy righteous

Humanistic ones
Thus is life and its plentiful twists

For colours are themselves your emotions
And it is up to you to envision these feelings
And their practical uses to you in your daily life
These words are written
For you to understand the harmony and the necessity of contradictions
The changing twists of emotions and their abstract sources
That are indefinable
No heaven shall save thee while you live on your earth
No choir, no opera shall rescue you
No saviour shall understand thee all
No martyr shall love you
No lover shall even think about you
No genius will ever comprehend your simplest formula
Only you
Will feel your entirety

The starting point of the foundation of one's existence
Is you being alone
As any nation stands alone
And in need of alliances and allies
Build therefrom
Build the tombs for your beliefs
Build the cathedrals for revolutionaries who are bloodied
Ye children of the sleepless nights
Awaken yourselves unto a reality that is more profound
Understand the criminals that swarm around you and within
Understand the masked atheistic priests who perpetually smile
Relate to the animals that wilfully ignore your existence

Think of your pitiful dreams
And your significant needs and what they mean to you
No one will care
I tell you
Life is the process of any Twilight
The existence of your autumn is arriving fast
The farewell cards and the farewell parties are not necessary
The eulogies and lies are for what?
For your body, mind and soul
That never found any peace amidst there endless
Pathetic civil war?
Do you know perhaps see

The face of death yawning at your puzzled face
Love death, expect death with passion

Do you look stupid?
Do you feel ugly?
Can you face that feeling?
Are you as ugly as embarrassment will take you?
Are you boring?
Are you an unwanted unit?
Are you aware of these condemnations of yourself?
Will you shrivel inside?
Is this your strength?
Is this the weight of your total bravery?
How much do you hate yourself and how much do you love yourself?
Do you want to know?
How much do you needs lovers to comfort you?

The truth is
Life cares naught for you
Humans care nothing for you
What does it matter if you were alive or not?
Wether you are a fierce soul and seemingly everlasting
And wether you have children multiplying
Your personal history
Transcends absolutely nothing
Remember that fact
And try to evolve your life
Therefrom.

About the Author

Ayad Gharbawi graduated from Boston University with an MA Degree in 1989 and went on to have his book, 'Conversations With Hitler And Stalin' published.